JOHN THE BAPTIST
IN-DEPTH, A CLOSER LOOK

JOHN THE BAPTIST
IN-DEPTH, A CLOSER LOOK

EVERETT AARON EDWARDS

A Division of WINEPRESS PUBLISHING

© 2006 by Everett Aaron Edwards. All rights reserved.

Pleasant Word (a division of WinePress Publishing, PO Box 428, Enumclaw, WA 98022) functions only as book publisher. As such, the ultimate design, content, editorial accuracy, and views expressed or implied in this work are those of the author.

No part of this publication may be reproduced, stored in a retrieval system or transmitted in any way by any means—electronic, mechanical, photocopy, recording or otherwise—without the prior permission of the copyright holder, except as provided by USA copyright law.

Unless otherwise noted, all Scriptures are taken from the Holy Bible, New International Version, Copyright © 1973, 1978, 1984 by the International Bible Society. Used by permission of Zondervan Publishing House. The "NIV" and "New International Version" trademarks are registered in the United States Patent and Trademark Office by International Bible Society.

Scripture references marked KJV are taken from the King James Version of the Bible.

Scripture references marked NASB are taken from the New American Standard Bible. © 1960, 1963, 1968, 1971, 1972, 1973, 1975, 1977 by The Lockman Foundation. Used by permission.

ISBN 1-4141-0697-1
Library of Congress Catalog Card Number: 2006901023

Table of Contents

Introduction VII

Chapter 1 – The Prophetic Call of John Before
He Was Born 11

Chapter 2 – The Childhood of John 31

Chapter 3 – Sell Everything You Have and Give to
the Poor and Come Follow Me! 51

Chapter 4 – Preacher, Teacher and Witness 63

Chapter 5 – Summary and Conclusion 75

Introduction

Many of you that have studied the Bible know him as John the Baptist. His Jewish birth name was Yochanan Ben Zechariah. We also know he lived as a wild man in the wilderness, ate locust and honey, and wore clothing made of camel hair. However, as careful Bible students, we also know that he was born to a well-off family at that time. This is because his father was an Aaronic priest, in the order of Abijah, as set by David the King.

We know that he preached and taught with a fervency that led people to think he was the Messiah, and this was done without the working of any miracles! He was said to be Elijah by spirit, even by the Lord Jesus, and again without doing any miracles. Many trusted

VIII JOHN THE BAPTIST IN-DEPTH: A CLOSER LOOK

in his word and as a result were baptized by him. And again, there was no evidence of who he was, nor any confirmation that he was of any account. In fact the opposite was known—that he was a madman preaching in the streets with a message that said: "Repent, for the kingdom of God is at hand," preparing for the coming of the Lord.

Why wasn't John living the same good life his father and mother lived? And what happened to his father's inheritance? Did John receive his father's inheritance? If not, then who did? We don't know if John was an only child. We do know he was the first son, but just as Abraham had other children, maybe John's father had other children. This is just a thought. Maybe John refused his father's inheritance.

His father's inheritance could have purchased a better life for John, where he would not have had to live as a wild man in the wilderness. His father was an Aaronic priest, and who knows whether the present high priest at that time, Caiaphas, had the same family genealogy going back to Aaron, the brother of Moses. All priests had to be a descendant of Aaron. It was believed that

Caiaphas may have purchased his position with money from the Romans, since this was going on by other officials at that time. Imagine the thought that John the Baptist or better, Yochanan Ben Zechariah, had a birthright that could have given him the office being held by the person who crucified the Lord Jesus, and that he was the Lord Jesus' cousin.

Was John the Baptist an Essene? Who were the Essenes and why even consider whether or not John was an Essene?

All these questions cannot be answered in this book, because there is no authenticated record. But this book will give revelation on some of these questions and will show how a man can be totally taken over by the Spirit of God. This book will show that John was completely taken over by God, and knowing this in itself answers most, if not all, these questions. Truly God was with John, and God was all that he had and by faith, God was all that he needed. With God, John did not need his father's inheritance, and maybe God told John not to take the inheritance.

X JOHN THE BAPTIST IN-DEPTH: A CLOSER LOOK

The objective of knowing as much about John the Baptist as we can learn is to know more about the Most High God and His Son, the Lord Jesus, and God's interaction in the lives of men.

Chapter 1

THE PROPHETIC CALL OF JOHN BEFORE HE WAS BORN

The Prophetic Call

John the Baptizer was called to be a prophet by God before he was born. The prophet Isaiah and the prophet Malachi, moving by the Spirit of God, prophesied about John's ministry hundreds of years before his birth. At the time of John's birth the angel Gabriel was sent to John's father, Zachariah, with a word from God. He gave them specific instructions to name the baby "John." He was not to drink strong drink, and he would be filled with the Holy Ghost at birth. The angel Gabriel also gave the purpose of John's ministry (Luke 1:13-17). Gabriel quoted Malachi saying, by *interpretation*, that

12 JOHN THE BAPTIST IN-DEPTH: A CLOSER LOOK

John was to introduce the Jewish Messiah, the messenger of the covenant, and that John would introduce this Jewish Messiah to Israel and to the whole world. Gabriel said that John would minister in the spirit and power of Elijah. And again Gabriel quoted Isaiah saying, by *interpretation*, that John would bring back many to the Lord their God, to turn the hearts of the fathers to their children and the disobedient to the wisdom of the righteous, to make ready a people prepared for the Messiah.

To understand the impact of John's ministry we need to understand that Gabriel used the name *Lord* (only the first letter of this word is capitalized), which in Hebrew means "Adonai." This is different from the name *Lord* (where all letters are capitalized), which in Hebrew means "Yah." We in Christendom accept Adonai as the Son of God, or Jesus, and of course Yah as God (see Psalm 110:1). Adonai in Psalm 110 is also interpreted as Messiah (Hebrew) or Christ (Greek). Jesus quoted this scripture in the gospels and Jesus used the name Christ or Messiah. Messiah and Christ are names Christian

The Prophetic Call of John Before He Was Born

theologians use for the Anointed One, the son of David, the Anointed King, the Son of the living God.

The angel Gabriel is first seen in scripture working as the angelic messenger of God when he was sent to the prophet Daniel, hundreds of years before John was born. In that event Gabriel called the Messiah, the Anointed One (Dan. 9:25). To recall that event: the messenger of God, Gabriel, appeared to the prophet Daniel at the end of his 21 days of fasting and prayer. Gabriel said he was first sent to Daniel when Daniel first started to pray, but was held up by the prince of the east (Dan. 10:13). In Gabriel's message he made the statement, "… to anoint the Most Holy" (Dan. 9:24). There are only two individuals in heaven that Gabriel could have been talking about as the Most Holy, because both are Most Holy. One is God the Father and the other is the Lord Jesus Christ, the Son of God. Now it's obvious that God the Father is not the Most Holy being talked about here, because no one in all creation is higher than God to anoint Him. Even Jesus said in the gospel of John: "The Father is greater than I" (John 14:28). Therefore, "the Most Holy" used in this scripture could have only been referring to the Lord Jesus Christ, and God the Father is the one who is anointing Him. We see this anointing being done in Daniel's night visions (Dan. 7:13). As a thought, we need to keep in mind that the price Jesus paid for His anointing came through His death, burial and resurrection (Isa. 53:10 and Rom. 1:4), and that through His anointing He purchased our redemption (Eph. 1:7).

We said earlier that John the Baptizer was prophesied by Isaiah and Malachi, and confirmed by the angel Gabriel. Of course later, John was also confirmed by Jesus Christ, Son of the living God. This confirmation is seen in Matthew 1:17, and by Christ in Matthew 11:14 and Luke 7:27. Isaiah prophesied that, "A voice of an unidentified person would cry out in the wilderness, saying prepare you the way of the LORD, make straight in the desert a highway for our God. Every valley shall be exalted, and every mountain and hill shall be made low and the rough places plain: And the glory of the LORD shall be revealed, and all flesh shall see together: For the mouth of the LORD has spoken" (Isa. 40:3). We know that this unidentified person Isaiah mentioned in this

The Prophetic Call of John Before He Was Born

scripture is John the Baptizer. We know this because of Gabriel's message to Zachariah, the father of John the Baptizer (Luke 1:17-19) and by the revealing words of Jesus Christ (Matt. 11:12-15) and by John himself when he was asked whom he was in the gospel of John. They all confirmed that John was the one spoken of by the prophet Isaiah (John 1:23).

Dual Prophecy

Malachi spoke of John in a dual prophetic word—that the time would come when God would send Elijah. This prophecy is called a dual prophecy because it rides on two levels. The first level is obvious because there was an actual living prophet named Elijah who lived in the flesh and was known for doing miracles and did not die, but was taken up to heaven in a chariot of fire (2 Kings 2:11). Therefore a direct interpretation is clear and informative, since it tells that this Elijah in the flesh would return to proclaim the coming of the Lord (the Messiah). But when Jesus said that John the Baptizer was Elijah in the spirit after John was in prison (Matt. 11:14), this gave a level of interpretation that could have only come from Heaven and Jesus, as the Son of God, did come from heaven (John 3:17). Gabriel, however, gave the same interpretation before John was born in Luke 1:16-17. Therefore, Jesus confirms Gabriel's message and both Jesus and Gabriel came from heaven. I believe that there is no way a person on earth could have known this. I also believe that John himself did not know this because when he was asked if he was Elijah he said, "I am not" (John 1:21).

It is theologically believed that Elijah in the flesh will return during an eschatological time. The New Testament book of Revelation tells of two prophets returning from heaven and one is believed by Christian theologians to be Elijah.

Another picture of a dual prophecy pertains to Jesus Himself. The Jewish rabbi community believes that Messiah in Daniel 9:25 is the LORD that comes from heaven to rule as king in Zechariah 14:9. But the same Jewish rabbi community does not believe that this is the same person in Isaiah 53 and Daniel 9:26a. They say that Isaiah is talking about Israel as a nation, suffering through

The Prophetic Call of John Before He Was Born

the years before receiving the promises of the scripture. However, by using the rule of duality in prophecy, as Jesus did with John the Baptist and Elijah, Christian theologians believe both are the same person. Christian theologians cite the story of Joseph where his suffering was used as a door to promote him to become Prime Minister of Egypt, second ruler only to Pharaoh. This is the same thing that happened to Jesus who suffered first and then became King (Heb. 2:10), second only to God the Father. Jesus said He was a King when Pilate asked him: "Are you a king?" (John 18:37).

John and Elijah

There are several similarities between John the Baptizer and Elijah. They both wore the same type of clothing—camel hair and a leather belt—giving them a similar appearance. And for a time Elijah ate directly from nature (meat given from ravens), while John ate locusts and honey. Elijah was known for miracles done by the Holy Spirit working through him, and John was known for the Word of God spoken by the Holy Spirit working through him. Elijah had little to say about the coming of Messiah, while John the Baptizer's sole purpose in life was to preach about His soon appearance and to point Him out.

Elijah performed seven miracles:

1. Food brought by ravens (1 Kings 17:5, 6)
2. Widow's food multiplied (1 Kings 17:12-16)
3. Widow's son raised to life (1 Kings 17:17-24)
4. Altar and sacrifice consumed (1 Kings 18:16-46)
5. Ahaziah's soldiers consumed (2 Kings 1:9-14)
6. Jordan River parted (2 Kings 2:6-8)
7. Transported to heaven (2 Kings 2:11, 12)

In contrast, John did no miracles but he was strong in the Holy Spirit and the Word of God. John spoke the Word of God with Holy Spirit power to the extent that he was even mistaken to be Messiah. But John the Baptizer proclaimed that he was not Messiah and the difference could be seen by the way he baptized. John said, "I indeed baptize you with water unto repentance: but he that cometh after me is mightier than I, whose

The Prophetic Call of John Before He Was Born

shoes I am not worthy to bear: he shall baptize you with the Holy Ghost, and with fire:" (Matt. 3:11).

We can see that God had given His Word the same level as His miracles. In fact, God's Word has a greater level than His miracles. God spoke through the prophet Jeremiah, "The prophet that hath a dream, let him tell a dream; and he that hath my word, let him speak my word faithfully. What is the chaff to the wheat? saith the LORD" (Jer. 23:28). In this scripture, God likened His miracles to chaff and His Word to wheat.

Chaff has no nourishment and/or worth and John said that it is thrown into the fire. But wheat gives nourishment and through its seeds it repeats the cycle of that nourishment and never stops. Also, the Lord said through the prophet Isaiah that God's Word comes down from heaven as rain and snow and gives nourishment to the seed and would not return to God void, but would do what God purposed it to do. Psalm 103:20 states that the angels hearken to the Word of God. And again the Lord said through David in Psalm 138:2b that "He had magnified His Word above all His Names."

JOHN THE BAPTIST IN-DEPTH: A CLOSER LOOK

Elijah must come first

Matthew, chapter 17, records that after the event on the Mount of Transfiguration Jesus tells the disciples not to tell anyone what had just happened until the Son of Man (meaning himself) had been raised from the dead. Transfiguration was an event involving a great open vision, but it left the disciples confused. And his disciples asked *Jesus*, saying, "Why then do *the teachers of the law* say that *Elijah* must first come?" And Jesus answered and said unto them, "*Elijah* truly shall come, and restore all things, But I say unto you, that *Elijah* is come already, and they knew him not, but have done unto him whatsoever they *wished*. Likewise shall also the Son of man suffer of them" (Matt. 17:10, *Rephrased*).

In this teaching we find two revelations: 1. "To be sure, Elijah comes and will restore all things..." and 2. Elijah has come already and they did not recognize him ..." The first revelation is a supporting scripture that gives credence to how a dual prophecy works. Notice that Jesus said, "To be sure Elijah comes and will restore all things." Jesus appears to be speaking of a future event.

The Prophetic Call of John Before He Was Born

The second revelation is a supporting scripture that John the Baptizer is Elijah (in the spirit), which is a current event at that time. This appears to be contradictory, but we know that God does not lie: "God is not a man that He should lie; neither the son of man, that he should repent: has He said and shall He not do it? Or has He spoken, and shall He not make it good?" (Num. 23:19). God also does not contradict himself: "For the Son of God, Jesus Christ, who was preached among you by us, even by me and Silvanus and Timotheus, was not yes and then no, but in Christ was yes. For all the promises of God in Christ are yes and in Christ Amen, unto the glory of God by us" (2 Cor. 1:19, 20). And Jesus said, "The scriptures cannot be broken" (John 10:35b). This is why the prophecy that "Elijah must come first and restore all things" is speaking of a two-level prophecy or a dual prophecy.

Only the Son of God could have given this illumination of Elijah because He came from God. Also Jesus confirms Gabriel's message that John would come in the spirit and power of Elijah. The reason the prophecy is called dual is because both are true. That means that

John the Baptizer is Elijah in the spirit to announce the Son of God's first coming and that Elijah in the flesh will come in the future to announce the Son of God's second coming. Remember, Elijah did his miracles by the Spirit of God and John had the Holy Spirit from birth, and we know that the Spirit of God does not lie. Therefore, the spirit of Elijah was in John the Baptizer, and that same spirit will come again in Elijah in the future.

Restore all things

What does it means to restore all things? Did John the Baptizer restore all things? Remember the prophecy that Isaiah gave in Isaiah 40:3: "The voice of him that crieth in the wilderness, Prepare ye the way of the LORD, make straight in the desert a highway for our God. Every valley shall be exalted, and every mountain and hill shall be made low; and the crooked shall be made straight, and the rough places plain: And the glory of the LORD shall be revealed, and all flesh shall see it together: for the mouth of the LORD has spoken it."

The Prophetic Call of John Before He Was Born

Notice the phrases, "the way of the Lord" and, "make straight in the desert a highway for our God" and, "Every valley shall be exalted, and every mountain and hill shall be made low" and "the rough places plain." These phrases, by interpretation, are a prophecy "to restore all things and prepare the way of the Lord" and are a call to live righteous and holy, because God is coming.

As a parallel, in time past God told Moses to tell his people to wash their clothes and stay away from their wives for three days, for on the third day they would see God. And again Moses told Aaron, after the death of his two sons Nadab and Abihu, that this was what the Lord meant when He said, "When you come near me you must treat me as holy." God requires holiness and righteousness before we come close. And by contrast the coming of Christ as Messiah, or as Son of God, is the same as the coming of God.

JOHN THE BAPTIST IN-DEPTH: A CLOSER LOOK

Gabriel's direct word from God

Earlier, I mentioned the angel Gabriel, the messenger of God, brought a word from heaven containing John the Baptist's birth and life, and it confirmed the prophecies of Isaiah and Malachi in Luke 1:5-20. The quote is as follows: "There was in the days of Herod, the king of Judea, a certain priest named Zachariah, of the course of Abia: and his wife was of the daughters of Aaron, and her name was Elisabeth. And they were both righteous before God, walking in all the commandments and ordinances of the Lord blameless. And they had no child, because that Elisabeth was barren, and they both were now well stricken in years. And it came to pass, that while he executed the priest's office before God in the order of his course, according to the custom of the priest's office, his lot was to burn incense when he went into the temple of the Lord. And the whole multitude of the people were praying outside the temple at the time of incense. And there appeared unto him an angel of the Lord standing on the right side of the altar of incense. And when Zachariah saw him, he was troubled, and

The Prophetic Call of John Before He Was Born

fear fell upon him. But the angel said unto him, Fear not, Zachariah: for thy prayer is heard; and thy wife Elisabeth shall bear thee a son, and thou shalt call his name John. And thou shalt have joy and gladness; and many shall rejoice at his birth. For he shall be great in the sight of the Lord, and shall drink neither wine nor strong drink; and he shall be filled with the Holy Ghost, even from his mother's womb. And many of the children of Israel shall he turn to the Lord their God. And he shall go before him in the spirit and power of Elias, to turn the hearts of the fathers to the children, and the disobedient to the wisdom of the just; to make ready a people prepared for the Lord. And Zachariah said unto the angel, Whereby shall I know this? for I am an old man, and my wife well stricken in years. And the angel answering said unto him, I am Gabriel, that stand in the presence of God; and am sent to speak unto thee, and to show thee these glad tidings. And, behold, thou shalt be dumb, and not able to speak, until the day that these things shall be performed, because thou believest not my words, which shall be fulfilled in their season."

Gabriel brought a direct word from God speaking of what was soon to come. This was an astonishing event that shows God working directly in the lives of men. Because Gabriel is not a man but an angel sent directly from the presence of God, there could be no doubt that this event would surely come to pass. An earthly parallel is like viewing an artist's picture of a building soon to be erected; when the building is finished, it looks exactly like the artist's picture. Gabriel's message ended the loss of hope for Zachariah and Elizabeth for ever giving birth to a son. After years of living righteously—praying for a son and believing God—now with Gabriel's message it was about to happen. This event lets Zachariah and Elizabeth know their prayers had been heard at first and now those prayers were about to be answered. The fact that they were well into their old age had to hurt a little, but God works in His own mysterious way.

Gabriel said that the boy child was to be named John. In Hebrew the name John is Yochanan which means, "God gives grace." Gabriel also brought the name *Jesus* from heaven to Mary the mother of Jesus the Son of God, which means, "God saves." Both names

The Prophetic Call of John Before He Was Born

together say, "God gives grace and God saves." Notice the statement, "And thou shalt have joy and gladness." This had to be supernaturally given because you don't have joy and gladness after waiting for a child so long that you're at an age where you're too old to enjoy the child and then have to go through the normal pains of childbirth. Childbirth is hard on young people, to say the least; how much more for old people. However, God kept Sarah beautiful and very attractive and although she was well stricken in old age, kings found her attractive and wanted her as their wife. God also kept Sarah healthy to have pleasure in her old age and even bear the son, Isaac. The angel Gabriel prophesied that John would give Zechariah and Elizabeth joy and gladness and that many would rejoice at his birth, as recorded in Luke 1:58: "Elizabeth's neighbors and relatives heard that the Lord had shown her great mercy, and they shared her joy." Also, Jesus said in John 5:35 that, "John was a lamp that burned and gave light, and the people chose for a time to enjoy his light." This confirmed Gabriel's message.

JOHN THE BAPTIST IN-DEPTH: A CLOSER LOOK

John was great in the sight of the Lord, just as Gabriel prophesied. Jesus reported this in Matthew 11:11: "Verily I say unto you, Among them that are born of women there has not risen a greater than John the Baptist." If John earned this great respect from Jesus, then we can be sure that John had earned the same great respect from God. When Gabriel told Zachariah that his son, John the Baptizer, "shall not drink neither wine nor strong drink, " this is similar to the Nazirite vows of a person dedicated to the service of God (see Num. 6:3). Likewise, John was dedicated to the service of the Lord his entire life, even to his death. The Bible has no record of John ever having personal enjoyment. Gabriel said that John would be filled with the Holy Ghost, even from his mother's womb. This is important because Jesus later said to his disciples that the Holy Ghost would be in them and later would be in the whole church. Elsewhere, Scripture says that this is to give the church the ministry of reconciliation (2 Cor. 5:18). John's preaching caused many to reconcile and repent and turn to God. John's preaching was so profound and powerful that many

The Prophetic Call of John Before He Was Born

mistook John the Baptizer for Christ (John 1:19). John was also mistaken for Elijah (John 1:22).

To conclude, the remainder of Gabriel's prophetic message from the Most High God in Heaven and the prophecy of Malachi and Isaiah were all fulfilled in the life of John the Baptist.

Chapter 2

THE CHILDHOOD OF JOHN

Bearing fruit in old age

"The righteous shall flourish like the palm trees: and he shall grow like a cedar in Lebanon. Those that he planted in the house of the LORD shall flourish in the courts of our God. They shall still bring forth fruit in old age; they shall be fat and flourishing; to show that the LORD is upright: he is my rock, and there is no unrighteousness in him" (Ps. 92:12-15).

This scripture was manifested in the lives of the parents of John the Baptist. John's parents were devout Jews and righteous before men and God. They were both well beyond childbearing age. They could have been in their thirties or forties. We know that Zechariah was not fifty, because he would have had to retire as required by Moses' instructions according to Numbers 8:25. Childbearing age then was very young—maybe between thirteen and twenty. Add the fact that they did not have modern medicine and many young women probably died in childbirth, for Elizabeth to have her first child at an old age and without complication is an even greater miracle.

Appropriate time

Modern medicine has allowed women to give birth in their fifties and even sixties, but not so for the first century. The birth of John the Baptist was a work of the miracles of God, similar to Abraham and Sarah. God brought forth John the Baptist at an appropriate time that existed only in the mind of God. This was because that time had a special meaning in the mind of God (Rom. 5:6). This was also a time when God would prove that He heard the prayers of John the Baptist's parents the first time they prayed, and even before they prayed.

The prophet Isaiah said the Lord promised that the time would come when "the Lord would answer before they call and while they were yet speaking" (Isa. 65:24).

This special time was known by God when He created the world. Paul mentions this in Ephesians: "According as He hath chosen us in Christ before the foundation of the world, that we should be holy and without blame before Him in love: Having predestinated us unto the adoption of children by Jesus Christ to Himself, according to the good pleasure of His will" (Eph. 1:4-5).

John was to prepare the way for the coming of the Lord Jesus Christ (Luke 1:17) and Jesus was hidden until His appearance, which was to take place at God's appointed time (Gal. 4:1-5). "But we speak the wisdom of God in a mystery, even the hidden wisdom, which God ordained before the world unto our glory; which none of the princes of this world knew, for had they known it, they would not have crucified the Lord of Glory" (1 Cor. 2:7-8).

God's ultimate plan is built on three pillars: 1.) Creation, 2.) Redemption, and 3.) Resurrection. God the Father initiated this plan with creation, the Son of God was next with redemption, and the next to come is the resurrection, with the Holy Spirit sealing the elect (Eph. 1:13-14). Of course Jesus is the central person of this plan in His redemptive work: "Who hath saved us, and called us with an holy calling, not according to our works, but according to his own purpose and grace, which was given us in Christ Jesus before the world began, But is now made manifest by the appearing of our Savior Jesus Christ, who hath abolished death, and hath brought life and immortality to light through the gospel" (2 Tim. 1: 9-10).

God's appointed time is similar to the germination of a seed. A seed has a reproductive structure in plants that consists of a plant embryo, usually accompanied by a supply of food (endosperm, which is produced during fertilization) and enclosed in a protective coat. Sprouting of a seed, or other reproductive body, usually occurs after a period of dormancy (or time) and absorption of water, and the availability of warming and oxygen and the exposure to light. All these are needed to operate in initiating the germination process.

In contrast, these properties are similar to the spiritual growth process. For instance:

1. Water is likened to the Word of God: "That he might sanctify and cleanse the church with the washing of water by the word" (Eph. 5:26).
2. Warming is likened to the fire of God: "For our God is a consuming fire" (Heb. 12:29).
3. Oxygen is likened to the wind of God or the Spirit of God: "And suddenly there came a sound from heaven as of a rushing mighty wind, and it filled all the house where they were sitting. And there appeared unto them cloven tongues like as of fire, and it sat upon each of them. And they were all filled with the Holy Spirit, and began to speak with other tongues" (Acts 2:4).
4. God Himself is light and He lives in the unapproachable light: "This then is the message which we have heard of him, and declare unto you, that God is light, and in him is no darkness at all" (John 1:5). "Who only hath immortality, dwelling in the light which no man can approach unto; whom no man hath seen, nor can see: to whom be honor and power everlasting. Amen" (1 Tim. 6:16). "Then spake Jesus

again unto them, saying, I am the light of the world: he that followeth me shall not walk in darkness, but shall have the light of life" (John 8:12).

For such a time as this

John's whole reason for living was to perform a Messianic mission—to announce the arrival of the Jewish Messiah or Adonah, also called the Lord (Isa. 52:10). Other prophets in the past announced the coming of the Lord, and not the immediate arrival of the Lord. This was to happen in John's lifetime, not far off in some future time; this was something totally new.

Messiah means the Anointed Prince, and John's mission was to point Him out. John used another name when the time came: "Behold the Lamb of God, which takes away the sins of the world." The name "Lamb of God" is used because God had promised in scripture to provide a sacrifice for the sin of the world, or the sin of Adam. This is given in the shadowy parable scripture, Gen. 3:15b: "… He shall bruise thy head, and thou shalt bruise his heel." Christian theologians for years have interpreted this as Christ's victory over the devil and atonement for sin by His redemptive work on Mount Calvary, which included His death, burial and resurrection. The theologian interpretation is that the devil bruised Christ's heel with His death and burial, but Christ bruised the devil's head with His resurrection and ascension, and is now seated in victory at the right hand of God the Father in heaven.

Peter said, "For you know that it was not with perishable things such as silver or gold that you were redeemed from the empty way of life handed down to you from your forefathers, but with the precious blood of Christ, a Lamb without blemish or defect. He was chosen before the creation of the world, but was revealed in these last times for your sake" (1 Pet. 1:18). This is a teaching in itself and outside the scope of this book. Notice John the Baptizer said "the sin" and not "the sin(s)," plural, meaning many. Christian theologians call this sin the sin of Adam which is the one sin that is the progeny of all sins in the world.

The term for such a time as this was used by Esther's uncle Mordecai (Es. 4:14) when he explained to

Esther what she needed to do to help save the Jews from Haman's plan to annihilate all the Jews. Haman had led King Xerxes to sign a decree that would eliminate all the Jews from the Persian Kingdom. Mordecai told Esther, who was the queen, not to acquiesce but to speak to the king even at the risk of losing her own life, in hopes the king would hear her and save the Jewish race. Esther, with the help of God, was successful, and Haman ended up being hung on the gallows that he intended for Mordecai.

The same expression, "for such a time as this", can be said for John the Baptist and more so for Christ (John 3:16). Esther did not lose her life, because God gave her favor with the king. The king heard her and delivered the Jews out of favor for Esther. But not so with Christ. Christ had to die to pay for our salvation. But after the price was paid, God (the King of creation) forgave our sins and saved our eternal lives from the devil's hell. And as Christ rose from the grave, so shall we.

Fellowship of the Holy Spirit

As earlier mentioned in this book, John was filled with the Holy Spirit at birth. This filling of the Holy Spirit at birth was important to develop an early fellowship and close walk with God. This is because John would later spend his early years, between ages 12 to 30, alone in the Judean desert. Age 12 is the age Jewish boys have their bar mitzvah (son of the law) and John's ministry is believed by theologians to have begun around the age of 30, the same age Jesus' ministry began.

The Holy Spirit was not given to John to perform miracles because John did no miracles (John 10:41), but to accurately hear from God, and to bear witness that Jesus is the Christ, the Son of the Living God, and to speak God's word flawlessly with Holy Spirit power. Remember that John had no formal training of the scriptures; he got his training directly from God. Evidence of this was when John, asked who he was, quoted Isaiah 40:3 perfectly. Also, the early filling of the Holy Spirit protected John from the enemy and the gainsayers. John's life was completely surrendered to God and there was no room for anything else in John's life but the will of God. The indwelling of the Holy Spirit at birth gave John a sound mind, and since he had no counselors, the Holy Spirit was his counselor.

Jesus said that when the Holy Spirit comes into a man that "he will reprove the world of sin, and of righteousness, and of judgment: Of sin, because they believe not on me; Of righteousness, because I go to my Father, and you see me no more; Of judgment, because the prince of this world (the devil) is judged" (John 16:8-11).

John was filled with the Holy Spirit at birth, but I believe these same words, which came years after John's birth, applied to John since God's words are timeless—past, present and future. John was six months older than Jesus (Luke 1:36) and Jesus was about 33 years of age at the time He spoke these words.

Aaronic priesthood; John's birthright

John's birthright made him an Aaronic priest because of the bloodline of his father, Zachariah. John the Baptizer's Jewish name is Yochanan Ben Zachariah, or John, son of Zachariah. Zachariah was an Aaronic priest in the order of Abijah (Luke 1:5 NIV). Abijah was a descendant of Ithamar, and Ithamar is a direct son of Aaron (1 Chr. 24:1-7, 10 NIV). Legally John had a right to be considered as a priest, and politically even to be appointed to the office of the high priest. Imagine that John could have had a right to the very office of the person that sentenced Jesus to death (John 11:50).

There is no record that John ever said anything about his priesthood birthright and whether or not he was disappointed that God had called him to a madman-like, prophetic ministry, as opposed to a glorified priesthood ministry. Of course Jesus mentions that a promotion in God is perceived to be a demotion to men, and a demotion in men is perceived to be a promotion to God.

Matthew said in his gospel: "If any man will come after me, let him deny himself, and take up his cross, and follow me. For whosoever will save his life shall lose it: and whosoever will lose his life for my sake shall find it" (Matt. 16:24, 25).

I said earlier that John was completely sold out for God and Christ. Remember, Jesus said to a rich man that he lacked one thing to obtain eternal life: "Sell everything you have and give to the poor and come follow me." Well, John is one person who has obeyed this commandment.

The Aaronic priesthood was different than the Levitical priesthood. The Levites were helpers under Aaron and his sons. Aaron and his sons were called of God to be priests throughout all generations, and the Levites and their sons were called by God to be their helpers. God told Moses to command Aaron and the Levites as follows: "This is the sum of the tabernacle, even of the tabernacle of testimony, as it was counted, according to the commandment of Moses, for the service of the Levites, by the hand of Ithamar, the son of Aaron the priest" (Ex. 38:21).

The Levites were to serve under Aaron the first priest and all the generations of his sons. Only the sons of Aaron were permitted to go into the Holy of Holies—offering incense, changing the holy bread, wicking the candelabra (or the menorah), and keeping it filled with oil.

God assured that Aaron's seed would be fruitful and that there would never be a shortage of sons of Aaron. However, to be the high priest you must be chosen by the sitting king. At the time of Christ, there was no son of David that came forward to be king, so they rotated the office yearly. John said in his gospel: "And they led Christ away to Annas first; for he was father-in-law to Caiaphas, which was the high priest that same year" (John 18:13).

Jewish rumors, for the first generation, were that the rotation of the office of high priest had to be purchased from the Romans. The tithes, gifts and revenue taken from the temple activities had to be shared between the high priest and the Romans. The high priest that could bring in the greatest amount of money won the acceptance and favor of the Romans and rewards for themselves.

They also cast lots for certain duties done by the priest as was done with Zechariah, the father of John the Baptist. Today it is believed that the Jews in Israel have authenticated approximately 5,000 sons of Aaron. There are two ways to be authenticated: one way is by legal papers and the other way is by Urim and Thummin (Num. 27:1). Urim and Thummin can only be done when the third temple is built and the high priest is ministering in Urim and Thummin inside the Holy of Holies. The Urim and Thummin is a form of divination where a question is put before the Lord that requires a "yes" or "no" answer. The Urim and Thummin is also called "tongues of fire" by Jewish tradition. The "tongues of fire" is used because two stones are used in the divination, one meaning "yes" and the other meaning "no." It is believed that the Lord would answer by lighting one of the stones, like lighting a fire. The actual process has been lost since the Babylonian captivity. Other methods are mentioned throughout Christendom, but this is just one.

"Tongues of fire" is likened to "cloven tongues as of fire" mentioned in the book of Acts (Acts 2:3). Therefore, tongues of fire could be said to be a kind of sign of the presence of the Holy Spirit. Also, Urim and

Thummin could be interpreted as the presence of the Holy Spirit.

Jesus is a unique Priest after the order of Melchizedec. The writer of Hebrews said: "Whither the forerunner is for us entered, even Jesus, made an high priest forever after the order of Melchizedec" (Heb. 6:20).

Jesus' priesthood is greater than Aaron's priesthood

Although this book is about John the Baptist, its main goal is to direct its readers to Christ, just as John's main goal was to direct Israel to Christ. Remember that John the Baptist's total existence on planet earth was to point Christ out.

We can never know everything about Christ; however, we know that He holds the office of Son of God, Son of Man, Prophet, Great High Priest in Heaven, and King of kings. Therefore, knowing a little about His priesthood is worth acknowledging. Hopefully we'll appreciate the office of priesthood for Aaron, and the priesthood that John had a right to, but never obtained.

In a way it also shows the mystery of God at work, since God chose John to be a prophet and not a priest.

The writer of Hebrews eloquently explained the difference between the priesthood of Aaron and the priesthood of Christ. Notice how much greater Christ's priesthood is over Aaron's priesthood: "For every high priest taken from among men is ordained for men in things pertaining to God, that he may offer both gifts and sacrifices for sins: Who can have compassion on the ignorant, and on them that are out of the way; for that he himself also is compassed with infirmity. And by reason hereof he ought, as for the people, so also for himself, to offer for sins. And no man takes this honor unto himself, but he that is called of God, as was Aaron. So also Christ glorified not himself to be made an high priest; but he that said unto him, Thou art my Son, today have I begotten thee. As he says also in another place, Thou art a priest forever after the order of Melchizedec. Who in the days of his flesh, when he had offered up prayers and supplications with strong crying and tears unto him that was able to save him from death, and was heard in that he feared; Though he were a Son, yet he learned obedience by the things which he suffered; And being made perfect, he became the author of eternal salvation unto all them that obey him; for He was called of God, an high priest after the order of Melchizedec" (Heb. 5:1-10).

John's childhood

John's childhood is not recorded in scripture except what we find in Luke 1:80: "And the child grew and became strong in spirit, and he lived in the desert until he appeared publicly." We don't know the age John left his parents' home and went into the Judean desert and we don't know what his parents had to say about him going to the desert or whether or not they were still living (remember that they were up in age when he was born). Jewish children are taught to obey their parents under the law of Moses. If John's parents were living and disapproved of him going into the desert at a young age (maybe the age of bar mitzvah), John would have had a dilemma between obeying God or obeying his parents. But we know God would not put him in this dilemma because God is not a God of confusion and this is the same God that gave Israel the law to obey their parents. Therefore it is suspected that John's parents were not living when he left and went into the Judean desert (at least not his father).

This is also true with Jesus. During the time of His ministry we never see His earthly father in scripture from ministry start to Jesus' death, so we have to conclude that Jesus' earthly father, Joseph, was not living at the start of His ministry. We also don't know if John had a tutor other than his father. This would be like a godfather that would look after John when his biological father passed on. Since John was under the direction of God, we have to conclude that God provided for John's care either supernaturally or through someone sent by God.

Was John an Essene?

The fact that John the Baptizer lived in the Judean desert until he appeared publicly brings the question to mind of whether John was an Essene. The Essenes were a group of people that lived in the desert alone as

THE CHILDHOOD OF JOHN   49

monks. They copied Scriptures and prayed at the times of the temple sacrifices and on a daily basis. They also practiced baptisms as part of their daily worship. Some Bible researchers believe that John studied under the Essenes and learned baptisms and the Scriptures from them, especially the book named Isaiah. For, as was said before, when John was asked who he was he quoted Isaiah 40:3 perfectly. A scroll of Isaiah was found in the Dead Sea scrolls during 1946-1947 written by the Essenes in the Dead Sea area of the Judean desert; this scroll was a perfect copy of the book Isaiah. Of course John's father could have taught John before he passed. Evidence for this is the word Gabriel had given to John's father concerning John before John's birth. John understood what the scriptures had to say about Messiah (Dan. 9:25a-26a), and Elijah (Mal. 4:5) and the prophet (Deut. 18:14-19). See John 1:19-23.

The Essenes dressed the same as John, wearing cloths like camel's hair with a leather belt, and ate as John—locust and honey. However there is no official record or archeological finding that proves John ever lived with the Essenes. Therefore we have to conclude that John was totally under God's care and alone in the desert. This was also true with Elijah; he lived alone in a cave and wore camel hair clothing with a leather belt and ate food that God supplied. God sent ravens bearing food to feed Elijah while he lived in a cave, hidden and protected until God was ready. He reappeared first to a widow woman who miraculously took care of him, and then before Ahab, the king of Israel, when it was time to do spiritual battle. I prefer to believe that John's father, Zachariah, repeated the scriptures concerning him from the message that Gabriel the angel of God gave him just before John's birth (Luke 1:11-20), and that Zachariah taught John the Scriptures concerning John, since his father was an Aaronic priest and a teacher of the Scriptures. Nevertheless, I choose to leave it a mystery.

Chapter 3

Sell Everything You Have and Give to the Poor and Come Follow Me!

John the Baptist was totally sanctified to God and for the Word of God from the time he leaped in his mother's womb to the time of his death. Again, John's name in Hebrew is Yochanan, which means, "Yahweh is gracious." Isn't it wonderful to know that the Lord is gracious toward all of us when we obey Him and are totally submitted to Him, and even at times when we don't obey Him? Many of us have not obeyed God and most of us have not obeyed Jesus' commandment to forsake all and follow Him (the main reason is probably because we would have to leave our financial comfort zone). This is a very hard thing to do, but John the Baptist did it and he was totally sanctified to God and

Christ from his birth to his death. Remember that John was brought up in the luxury of the home of an Aaronic priest, Zachariah his father. Zachariah had the income to live very well for that time. So John knew the difference between comfort and discomfort. When John left his parents' home and went into the Judean desert he knew he was giving up comfort for discomfort. But John trusted God to provide. Imagine going from eating choice meat brought to the temple for sacrificial offering (Lev. 7:31-36), to locust and honey found in the wild.

Jesus said if we seek our life we will lose our life, but if we lose our life for the kingdom of God we will find our life. As it was elaborately said in scriptures, "Then said Jesus to his disciples, If any man will come after me, let him deny himself, and take up his cross, and follow me. For whosoever will save his life shall lose it but whoever loses his life for my sake shall find it. For what profit is it to a man if he gains the whole world and loses his own soul? Or what will a man give in exchange for his soul? For the Son of man shall come in the glory of his Father and with his angels; and then he shall reward every man according to his works" (Matt. 16:24-27).

Sell Everything You Have and Give to the Poor and Come Follow Me!

Elsewhere Jesus said, "It is the Spirit that gives life; the flesh profits nothing; The words that I speak unto you, they are spirit, and they are life" (John 6:63). And Paul added later: "Now the Lord is that Spirit: and where the Spirit of the Lord is, there is liberty" (2 Cor. 3:17).

Therefore, by being submitted to the Lord Jesus, we find our lives, we are rewarded upon Jesus' second coming, we obtain life (eternal life), and we obtain liberty!

A rich young man came to Jesus seeking eternal life and Jesus instructed the man to sell everything he had and give to the poor and come follow Him. The rich man could not do this and the Bible said he walked away sorrowful. We know this is a commandment of the Lord to the church to sell everything they have and give to the poor and come and follow Him—because God never suggests, He commands. This is true of Sister Teresa in Calcutta, India, and many others like her around the world, and some of you readers who have obeyed this commandment and therefore understand John the Baptist's position fully.

Giving to the poor is also concomitant with giving to the Church. When Israel came out of Egypt, God blessed the people so they were able to give to Moses for the building of the tabernacle and for the support of the priests and Levites who worked and serviced the tabernacle.

I grew up poor and destitute and find this commandment extremely hard to do, but I try not to be stingy. I do give what I have the faith to give. However, John the Baptist's entire life was in total surrender and obedience to this commandment. Remember that John's birthright was in the line of the Aaronic priesthood, yet there is no record where John ever grumbled that he had the right to be a priest and should not be living in the wild like a madman.

The Apostles obeyed this commandment. Remember that Peter and his brother, Andrew, and their partners, James and John, were fishermen and had at least two boats (Luke 5:7). Owning two boats shows that they had prospered, or better yet, that God had prospered them. And Matthew was a tax collector. But when Jesus said to Peter and company, "Follow me and I'll make

Sell Everything You Have and Give to the Poor and Come Follow Me!

you fishers of men," and to Matthew to "come follow me," they all left their professions and followed Jesus. Amen. Now that's faith in action. I'm not sure I could have done that.

Following Jesus has greater rewards than earthly rewards

"Then Peter began to say to the Lord Jesus Christ; Lord, we have left all, and followed you. And Jesus answered and said, verily I say unto you, There is no man that hath left house, or brethren, or sisters, or father, or mother, or wife, or children, or lands, for my sake and the gospel sake and not be rewarded, but anyone that does leave house, or brethren, or sisters, or father, or mother, or wife, or children, or lands, for my sake and the gospel sake shall receive hundredfold now in this time, houses, and brethren, and sisters, and mothers, and children, and lands, but with persecutions; and in the world to come eternal life" (Mark 10:28-31).

Sometimes the reward from following Jesus is not apparent. You have to move in the Spirit by faith to see it and receive it. You can see this working with the following scripture: "….unless you eat the flesh of the Son of Man and drink his blood, you have no life in you" (John 6:53b). We must understand that Moses had earlier said that drinking blood would bring a curse (Lev. 17:10). Jesus knew the Law of Moses better than anyone on planet earth; in fact, He knew the law better than Moses himself. This is because of His office as Son of God, sent from heaven, and He never intended to break the Law of Moses. If Jesus had broken the Law of Moses he would have been a transgressor of the law, and thereby a sinner. This would have made Him unacceptable as a sacrifice for sin. In fact, He Himself would have needed a sacrifice for sin.

Then why did Jesus use this type of language knowing that it would enrage the Jewish listeners but not those given to Him by God the Father? Many of the listeners said, "This is a hard saying and who can bear it." The writer said that many left Him and followed Him no more. But when Jesus asked the twelve, "Will you go too?" Peter said, "To whom shall we go? You have the words of eternal life. And we believe and are sure that you are that Christ, the Son of the living God." Peter and the twelve moved by faith, and even though they could not understand Jesus' hard words, they still stood with Jesus. But notice that the reward here was eternal life.

Jesus did not mean to drink actual blood because Jesus did no sin (2 Corinthians 5:21). If He had, He could not have been our propitiation for our sins (Rom. 3:25, 1 John 2:2, and 1 John 4:10). Jesus knew the Law of Moses better than they, and He did not break the law. What Jesus was doing was separating the goats from the sheep (John 10:26-29) and setting up communion and things to do to observe communion: "Do this in remembrance of me" (Matt. 26:26-28). This separation was because some people were never meant to know certain things of God, because they were never meant to be partakers of Jesus.

Jesus explained this mystery to His disciples when He explained the understanding of the mystery of the sower: "And the disciples came, and said unto him, Why speakest thou unto them in parables? He answered and said unto them, Because it is given unto you to know the mysteries of the kingdom of heaven, but to them it is not given. For whosoever hath, to him shall be given, and he shall have more abundance: but whosoever hath not, from him shall be taken away even that he hath. Therefore speak I to them in parables: because they seeing see not; and hearing they hear not, neither do they understand. And in them is fulfilled the prophecy of Esaias, which saith, By hearing ye shall hear, and shall not understand; and seeing ye shall see, and shall not perceive: For this people's heart is waxed gross, and their ears are dull of hearing, and their eyes they have closed; lest at any time they should see with their eyes and hear with their ears, and should understand with their heart, and should be converted, and I should heal them. But blessed are your eyes, for they see: and your ears, for they hear" (Matt. 13:10-16).

John the Baptist received no reward on planet earth except to do the will of God the Father and to point out Jesus the Christ, the Lamb of God. John had no earthly possessions that were mentioned in Scripture. Ever wonder what happened to the belongings that John's father Zachariah had acquired in his life, and why John the Baptist didn't inherit them? The Bible never mentions

Sell Everything You Have and Give to the Poor and Come Follow Me!

an earthly inheritance for John. In fact, the Bible mentions John spending all his time baptizing, preaching, teaching, and judging Herod for God the Father. The food John ate cost him nothing since he ate locusts and honey that God provided free in nature. John was totally surrendered to God.

Even Paul said "amen" to this commandment. Paul writes, "But what things were gain to me, those I counted loss for Christ. Yea doubtless, and I count all things but loss for the excellency of the knowledge of Christ Jesus my Lord; for whom I have suffered the loss of all things, and do count them but dung, that I may win Christ ..." (Phil. 3:7-8).

The act of surrender must be complete to be rewarded. A man said to Jesus, "Lord I will follow you; but let me first go bid them farewell, who are at my house. And Jesus said unto him, No man, having put his hand to the plow, and looking back, is fit for the kingdom of God" (Luke 9:61, 62). At another place in scripture Jesus said, "Remember Lot's wife," and again, "Whosoever shall seek to save his life shall lose it; and whosoever shall lose his life shall preserve it" (Luke 17:33). And elsewhere, the Bible says, "For it is impossible for those who were once enlightened, and have tasted of the heavenly gift, and were made partakers of the Holy Spirit, and have tasted the good word of God, and the powers of the age to come, If they shall fall away, to renew them again unto repentance; seeing they crucify to themselves the Son of God afresh, and put him to an open shame" (Heb. 6:4-6).

John's humiliation

John was beheaded by Herod the king to please his wife. She, probably being demonically possessed, subsequently became convicted from John's preaching. John was preaching against her marriage to King Herod because she was married to his brother. John's beheading was a type of satanic humiliation before God the Father, similar to the crucifixion of Christ. It wasn't enough for Satan to kill John; he had to humiliate him in his death. The same was true with Christ. Christ was crucified almost naked. Nakedness before God is a type of humiliation. It wasn't enough to kill Jesus; the devil wanted to humiliate God the Father at the same time. The following are the supporting scriptures: "Neither shalt thou go up by steps unto mine altar, that thy nakedness be not discovered thereon" (Ex. 20:26).

"And thou shalt make them linen breeches to cover their nakedness; from the loins even unto the thighs they shall reach" (Ex. 28:42).

The day will come when that which the devil meant for evil will be turned for good, even the beheading of John and others for the Gospel of Jesus Christ. Just as Jesus was promoted after His humiliation on the cross, so will those beheaded for God be promoted in heaven: "And I saw thrones, and they sat upon them, and judgment was given unto them: and I saw the souls of them that were beheaded for the witness of Jesus, and for the word of God, and which had not worshipped the beast, neither his image, neither had received his mark upon their foreheads, or in their hands; and they lived and reigned with Christ a thousand years" (Rev. 20:4).

Chapter 4

Preacher, Teacher and Witness

John as the preacher

As it is written in the prophets (Malachi and Isaiah), "Behold, I send my messenger before your face; he shall prepare your way before these people. He will be the voice of one crying in the wilderness, saying prepare the way of the Lord; make His paths straight." This messenger or forerunner of Christ is John Ben Zachariah, or better known as John the Baptizer. He came into all the country about Jordan, preaching the baptism of repentance for the remission of sins; and saying that all flesh shall see the salvation of God.

John's preaching began in the wilderness of Judea. He went into all the land, "And saying, Repent *you*: for the kingdom of heaven is at hand" (Matt. 3:2, *Rephrased*). "But when *John* saw many of the Pharisees and Sadducees come to his baptism, he said unto them, "Oh *you* generation of vipers, who *have* warned you to flee from the wrath to come?" (Matt. 3:7, *Rephrased*).

"Bring forth therefore *reports showing you are worthy of* repentance: and think not to say within yourselves, we have Abraham *as* our father: *and therefore deserve to be baptized for repentance of sins*. For I say unto you, that God is able *to raise these stones* up *to be* children *of* Abraham. And now also the axe is laid unto the root of the trees: therefore every tree which *does not bring* forth good fruit (*meaning good deeds*) is *cut* down, and cast into the fire" (Matt. 3:8-10, *Rephrased*).

However, the mercy of God working through Christ can be seen in a parable that *Jesus told about a vineyard owner who told a worker in his vineyard to cut down a tree which was not producing fruit; the vineyard worker answered and said, "Let me fertilize it and next year if it does not produce fruit then I'll cut it down"* (Luke 13:6-9,

Rephrased). This parable shows Jesus as priest making intercession between God and us, as the scriptures say that mercy and truth came by Jesus Christ. "Wherefore he is able also to save them to the uttermost that come unto God by him, seeing he ever *lives* to make intercession for them" (Heb. 7:25, *Rephrased*).

John said that, "*he* indeed baptize *a person* with water unto repentance: but he that cometh after me is mightier than I, whose shoes I am not worthy to bear: He shall baptize you with the Holy Ghost, and with Fire: Whose fan is in his hand, and he will thoroughly purge his *thrashing* floor, and gather his wheat into the garner; but he will burn up the chaff with unquenchable fire" (Matt. 3:12, *Rephrased*).

John also preached righteousness to King Herod for taking his brother's wife. John's preaching to King Herod is similar to Amos's preaching to King Jeroboam of Israel for worshipping another god. Both prophets showed fearless boldness before kings that were wayward to the commandments of God. Both kings were afraid of these two prophets. With John, King Herod was tricked by his illegal wife to have John imprisoned and finally put to death. King Jeroboam never overcame his fear of Amos but invited him to leave Israel and go back to Judah.

John as the teacher

And the people responded and asked John, saying to him, what shall we do then? John taught by saying to them, "He that has two coats, let him give to him that has no coat; and he that has food, let him do likewise. Then came the publicans also to be baptized, and said to John, Master, what shall we do? And he said unto them, Exact no more than that which is appointed you. And the soldiers likewise demanded of him, saying, And what shall we do? And he said to them, do violence to no man, neither accuse any falsely; and be content with your wages. John taught as Jesus did, almost as if they had the same the teacher. Many at that time felt that both Jesus and John had been taught by the rabbi sage of that time, such as Shammai. Rabbi Shammai differed from Rabbi Hillel in that Shammai had interpreted scripture strictly and Hillel interpreted scripture

Preacher, Teacher and Witness

loosely. There was a saying at that time that Shammai bound and Hillel loosed. Jesus' favorite book in scripture was Deuteronomy. Jesus used it often. The book of Deuteronomy is the second giving of the Law by Moses. Moses wanted to drive home the judgment of God, the fear of God, the wrath of God, the goodness of God, and the blessings of God, and that favor with God comes from obedience of God.

Jesus and John taught similar messages, "Repent for the kingdom of God is at hand." John the Baptist puts one in mind of Amos. Amos taught that the Lord said: "For thus saith the LORD unto the house of Israel, Seek ye me, and ye shall live: But seek not Bethel, nor enter into Gilgal, and pass not to Beersheba: for Gilgal shall surely go into captivity and Bethel shall come to nought. Seek the LORD, and ye shall live; lest he break out like fire in the house of Joseph, and devour it, and there be none to quench it in Bethel. Ye who turn judgment to wormwood, and leave off righteousness in the earth, Seek him that maketh the seven stars and Orion, and turneth the shadow of death into the morning, and maketh the day dark with night: that calleth for the waters of the sea, and poureth them out upon the face of the earth: The Lord is his name: That strengtheneth the spoiled against the strong, so that the spoiled shall come against the fortress. They hate him that rebuketh in the gate, and they abhor him that speaketh uprightly. Forasmuch therefore as your treading is upon the poor, and ye take from him burdens of wheat: ye have built houses of hewn stone, but ye shall not dwell in them; ye have planted pleasant vineyards, but ye shall not drink wine of them. For I know your manifold transgressions and your mighty sins: they afflict the just, they take a bribe, and they turn aside the poor in the gate from their right. Therefore the prudent shall keep silence in that time; for it is an evil time. Seek good, and not evil, that ye may live: and so the Lord, the God of hosts, shall be with you, as ye have spoken. Hate the evil, and love the good, and establish judgment in the gate: it may be that the Lord God of hosts will be gracious unto the remnant of Joseph. Therefore the Lord, the God of hosts, the Lord, saith thus; Wailing shall be in all streets; and they shall say in all the highways, Alas! alas! and they shall call the husbandman to mourning, and such as are skillful of lamentation to wailing. And in all vineyards shall be wailing: for I will pass through thee, saith the LORD. Woe unto you that desire the day of the LORD! to what end is it for you? the day of the LORD is darkness, and not light. As if a man did flee from a lion, and a bear met him; or went into the house, and leaned his hand on the wall, and a serpent bit him. Shall not the day of the LORD be darkness, and not light? even very dark, and no brightness in it? I hate, I despise your feast days, and I will not smell in your solemn assemblies. Though ye offer me burnt offerings and your meat offerings, I will not accept them: neither will I regard the peace offerings of your fat beasts. Take thou away from me the noise of thy songs; for I will not hear the melody of thy viols. But let judgment run down as waters, and righteousness as a mighty stream" (Amos: 5: 4-24).

John as the baptizer of Christ

"And as the people were in expectation, and all men mused in their hearts of John, whether he *was* the Christ or not; *They asked John if he was the Christ, or not; and*

"John answered, saying unto them, I indeed baptize you with water; but one mightier than I *will come*, the latchet of his shoes I am not worthy to unloose. He shall baptize you with the Holy Ghost and with fire: Whose fan is in *his* hand, and he will thoroughly purge his threshing floor, and will gather the wheat into his garner; but the chaff he will burn with *unquenchable fire.*" *And John preached many other things such as* this in his exhortation *to* the people (Luke 3:15-18, *Rephrased*).

Sign for John to know Jesus was the Son of God

God gave John a specific signal that would point out the Christ. John said he did not know Him except that He who sent him to baptize (God) said that the one who would baptize with the Holy Ghost would receive power from God, without measure, when the Holy Ghost in the form of a dove came upon Him and would not depart. John the apostle added that the Holy Ghost was given to Christ without measure.

Peter said in Acts 10:38 that God anointed Jesus with the Holy Ghost and with power and that Jesus went about doing good and healing all that were oppressed of the devil, for God was with Him. And we, the Church, would know Him the way John the Baptist said we would know Him—after He baptizes us with the Holy Ghost.

The first time John saw Jesus coming to be baptized, he forbad him *and said to Jesus*, "I have need to be baptized of *you* and *you* come to me?" And Jesus answering, said unto him, "Suffer it be so now: for we must fulfill all righteousness." Then *John* suffered him, (Matt. 3:13-15, *Rephrased*).

John's last witness of Christ

"John the Baptist was a man sent from God. The same came for a witness, to bear witness of the light that all men through him might believe. He was not that light, but was sent to bear witness of that Light. That was the true Light, which lights every man that *comes* into the world" (John 1:6-9, *Rephrased*).

"John bare witness of *Jesus*, and cried, saying, this was he of whom I *spoke*, He that *came* after me is preferred before me: for he was before me. And of his fullness have we all received, and grace for grace. For the law was given to Moses, but grace and truth came by Jesus Christ.

No man *has* seen God at any time; the only begotten Son, which is in the bosom of the Father, he has declared him" (John 1:15-18, *Rephrased*).

"And this is the record of John, when the Jews sent priests and Levites from Jerusalem to ask him, who *are you?* And John confessed, and denied not; but confessed, I am not the Christ. And they asked him, what then? Are you *Elijah?* And he said, I am not. Are you that prophet? And he answered, no. Then said they unto him, who are you? That we may give an answer to them that sent us. What *say you* of yourself? John said, I am the voice of one crying in the wilderness, Make straight the way of the Lord, as said the prophet Isaiah.

And they which were sent were of the Pharisees. And they asked *John*, and said unto him, why baptizest *you* then, if *you* be not that Christ, nor *Elijah*, neither that prophet? John answered them, saying, I baptize with water: but there *stands* one among you, whom *you* know not; He it is, *who's* coming after me is preferred before me, whose shoe's latchet I am not worthy to unloose. These things were done in Bethabara beyond Jordan, where John was baptizing" (John 1:20-28, *Rephrased*).

The next day John saw Jesus coming unto him, and said, Behold the Lamb of God, which *takes* away the sins of the world. This is He of whom I said, After me *comes* a man which is preferred before me: for He was before me. And I knew Him not: but that He should be made manifest to Israel, therefore am I come baptizing with water. And John bare record, saying, I saw the Spirit descending from heaven like a dove, and it abode upon him *and not departed* (John 1:29-32, *Rephrased*).

> **And I knew Him not: but He that sent me to baptize with water, the same said unto me, Upon Whom thou shalt see the Spirit descending, <u>and remaining on Him</u>, the same is He which baptizeth with the Holy Ghost.**
> **And <u>I saw and bare record that this is the Son of God</u>.**
> **(John 1:33-34)**

"Again the next day after John stood, and two of his disciples; Again looking upon Jesus as he walked, he said, Behold the Lamb of God! And the two disciples heard him speak, and they followed Jesus" (John 1:35-36, *Rephrased*).

John continued to witness of Christ knowing his ministry was over (or that is to say; his mission has been completed)....He must increase while I must decrease.

Chapter 5

Summary and Conclusion

The office of a prophet is to herald a soon-to-occur event of God (Amos 3:7). The prophet is to speak only of that event and not about himself/herself (John 15:26-27; Rev. 19:10). The prophet is to teach the people how to prepare themselves for the event (1 Cor. 14:3). The event must happen to authenticate the prophet and the prophet's relationship with God, since God is the only one that can bring the event to pass (Deut. 18:22). However an event can occur and the prophet still not be authentic (Deut. 13:1-5, John 15:26). The test in these cases is to observe the message that the prophet speaks. The prophet must speak only the message to follow God and Christ. It is the Spirit of God that gives the prophet his ability, and all prophets move and speak by the Spirit of God. The spirit of prophesy is the testimony of Jesus Christ, and the Lord is the Spirit and where the Spirit of the Lord is, there is liberty. Jesus also said to observe the fruit of a prophet. Some prophets perform miracles and some have the Word of God only. The greater power is in God's Word; the miracles are signs to confirm the Word of God. The prophet speaks God's words with power emanating from the anointing of the Holy Ghost.

John the Baptist fulfilled the office of a prophet perfectly from the time he was filled with the Holy Spirit while still in his mother's womb to the time he asked Christ through his disciples, because John was imprisoned by Herod: "Are you the one or shall we look for another?" The Bible said Jesus did many miracles in that same hour; He healed sick folks, cast out demons, gave sight to the blind, made the lame walk, gave speech to the dumb and hearing to the deaf, the dead were raised, and the poor were preached to. By these actions, Jesus was proving to John that He was the Messiah, the Son of David, and the Son of God. Then Jesus told John's disciples to go tell John what they had seen and to say,

"Blessed is he that is not offended in me." Many people say that this action of John displayed that John was losing faith in Jesus. They forgot that the Messiah was to be a prophet like Moses and John knew this. Remember Moses spent time with God on the mountain and came down from the mountain performing miracles as reason for Pharaoh to let God's people go. I propose that John was not losing faith but that he was losing patience. In fact, John had a lot of faith implanted in him as one of the gifts of the indwelling of the Holy Spirit (1 Cor. 12:9). But I believe that John was wondering why Jesus had not gone to Pilate and Herod and said as Moses said, "The LORD said to let my people go." I believe that John was asking Jesus to use His miracles like Moses used miracles to get him out of jail and get on with the business of getting rid of the Romans and Herod and returning Israel to the Davidic kingdom in all its glory as prophesied in Deuteronomy 18:15.

A sobering point to make is that John knew his life and ministry was over when Jesus sent His answer and added something close to a rebuke: "Blessed are those that are not offended in me." In plain words, Jesus was saying, "I will do more miracles to heal, cast out the devils, etc., but no, I will not get you out of jail and you should remain faithful and not be offended with me." John knew it was God's will for him to die in Herod's prison. The Bible gives no record of John complaining or murmuring, but only silence and his total surrender to God and Christ even to his death. Prior to John's imprisonment he said at one time, "I must decrease so he can increase."

John's ministry was so effective that many of his disciples continued to serve him and to continue in his teachings and did not convert to Jesus' ministry until they were directly confronted by the Apostles. As a record of proof, there was a man named Apollos who was eloquent and mighty in the Scriptures and he knew only the baptism of John (Acts 18:24-26). Plus the saints at Ephesus knew, too, only the baptism of John (Acts 19:1-7).

The life of Jesus Christ on planet earth cannot be told in detail without first beginning with the life of John the Baptist. The writer of the book of Acts mentions John as the starting point of the apostles' call to follow Christ. This, too, gives proof of the effectiveness that the prophetic ministry of John the Baptist did an excellent job for God and the Lord Jesus Christ.

Jesus' confirmation of John as a prophet

John was accepted as a prophet by many and they came in great numbers to hear John preach, teach and to be baptized. When they came to John they had to trouble themselves in travel, since John was in the desert and not in the city. They confirmed John as a prophet by overcoming these obstacles to be ministered to by John in the desert. Jesus recalls it in the following scriptures: "You sent unto John, and he bare witness unto the truth. But I receive not testimony from man: but these things I say, that you might be saved. He was a burning and a shining light: you were willing for a season to rejoice in his light" (John 5:33-35).

"Therefore they sought again to take him: but he escaped out of their hand, and went away again beyond Jordan into the place where John at first baptized; and there he abode. And many resorted unto him, and said, John did no miracle: but all things that John spoke of this man were true" (John 10:39-41).

"And as they departed, Jesus began to say unto the multitudes concerning John, what went you out into the wilderness to see? A reed shaken with the wind? But what went you out for to see? A man clothed in soft raiment? Behold, they that wear soft clothing are in kings' houses. But what went you out for to see? a prophet? Yes, I say unto you, and more than a prophet, for this is he of whom it is written; Behold, I send my messenger before your face, which shall prepare your way before me. Verily I say unto you, among them that are born of women there has not risen a greater prophet than John the Baptist: notwithstanding he that is least in the kingdom of heaven is greater than he. And from the days of John the Baptist until now the kingdom of heaven suffers violence, and the violent take it by force. For all the prophets and the law prophesied until John. And if you will receive it, this is Elijah, which was to come" (Matt. 11:7-14).

John's final testimony of Christ and how it shows ultimate humiliation

Question: What does a prophet do when God has brought his ministry to an end and he knows it? Answer: Continue in that calling until you hear from God. A supporting scripture is 1 Corinthians 7: 20-24: "You should continue on as you were when God called you. Are you a slave? Don't let that worry you—but if you get a chance to be free take it. And remember, if you were a slave when the Lord called you, the Lord has now set you free from the power of sin. And if you were free when the Lord called you, you are now a slave of Christ. Christ purchased you with a high price. So brethren, whatever situation you were in when God called you, stay there with God."

God calls a prophet to a ministry and God ends his ministry. John knew his ministry was over but he continued to baptize the people. John was called as follows: to be a forerunner for Christ and to point Him out and he did that; John was told to make straight the way of the Lord and he did that through his preaching and teaching. John was looking for new directions from God, but none came and the Bible records the situation in John 3:22-36 leading up to John's imprisonment and subsequently his death.

Notice John's strength and faith in the Holy Ghost: "After these things came Jesus and his disciples into the land of Judea; and there he tarried with them, and baptized. And John also was baptizing in Aenon near to Salim, because there was much water there: and they came, and were baptized. For John was not yet cast into prison. And they came unto John, and said unto him, Rabbi, he that was with you beyond Jordan, to whom you barest witness, behold, the same baptizeth, and all men come to him. John answered and said, a man can receive nothing, except it be given him from heaven. You yourselves bear me witness, that I said, I am not the Christ, but that I am sent before him. He that has the bride is the bridegroom: but the friend of the bridegroom, which stands and hears him, rejoices greatly because of the bridegroom's voice: this my joy therefore is fulfilled. He must increase, but I must decrease" (John 3:22-30).

John, the writer of the gospel of John, continued with the following words: "He that comes from above is above all: he that is of the earth is earthly and speaks of the earth: He that comes from heaven is above all. And what he has seen and heard, that he testifies; and no man receives his testimony. He that has received his testimony has set to his seal that God is true. For he whom God has sent speaks the words of God: for God gives not the Holy Ghost by measure unto him. The Father loves the Son, and has given all things into his hand. He that believes on the Son has everlasting life: and he that believes not on the Son shall not see life; but the wrath of God abides on him" (John 3:31-36).

John's request to Jesus was similar to Jesus' request to God the Father

When John told his disciples to ask Jesus if he was the one or should they look for another, it was similar to Jesus asking God the Father to let this cup pass from Him. But just as John accepted Jesus' will, which led him to be beheaded, Jesus accepted God the Father's will, which led to Him being crucified. John ultimately was humiliated by being beheaded. John's beheading has a special place with God and Christ as documented in Revelation 20:4: "And I saw thrones, and they sat upon them, and judgment was given unto them: and I saw the souls of them that were beheaded for the witness of Jesus, and for the word of God, and which had not worshipped the beast, neither his image, neither had received his mark upon their foreheads, or in their hands; and they lived and reigned with Christ a thousand years."

John the Baptist is obviously enjoying great blessings in heaven, and everything he never had on planet earth he's getting more than he could have imagined: "Eyes have not seen and ears have not heard what God has planned for those that love Him" (1 Cor. 2:9). Saints of God, we need to learn from John the Baptist to serve God as he did and not ourselves.

From the time of John the Baptist until now, the Kingdom of God suffers violence and the violent take it by force (Matt. 11:12).

To order additional copies of this title call:
1-877-421-READ (7323)
or please visit our web site at
www.pleasantwordbooks.com

CPSIA information can be obtained at www.ICGtesting.com
Printed in the USA
LVOW131445160513

334165LV00001B/115/A